The Bizarre History of Beauty

TERRIBLE AND TOXIC MAKEUP

ANITA CROY

 Gareth Stevens
PUBLISHING

Please visit our website, www.garethstevens.com.
For a free color catalog of all our high-quality books,
call toll free 1-800-542-2595 of fax 1-877-542-2596.

Cataloging-in-Publication Data
Names: Croy, Anita.
Title: Terrible and toxic makeup / Anita Croy.
Description: New York : Gareth Stevens Publishing, 2019. | Series: The bizarre history of beauty | Includes
glossary and index.
Identifiers: ISBN 9781538226773 (pbk.) | ISBN 9781538226766 (library bound)
Subjects: LCSH: Beauty, Personal–Juvenile literature. | Beauty culture–Juvenile literature. | Cosmetics–Juvenile
literature. | Cosmetics–History–Juvenile literature.
Classification: LCC RA777.C79 2019 | DDC 646.7′2–dc23

First Edition

Published in 2019 by
Gareth Stevens Publishing
111 East 14th Street, Suite 349
New York, NY 10003

© 2019 Gareth Stevens Publishing

Produced for Gareth Stevens by Calcium
Editors: Sarah Eason and Tim Cooke
Designers: Clare Webber and Lynne Lennon
Picture researcher: Rachel Blount

Picture credits: Cover: Shutterstock: Sergii Rudiuk; Inside: Library of Congress: Esther Bubley: p. 36;
Shutterstock: ArgenLant: p. 7b; Steve Boice: p. 13; S. Borisov: p. 20; Buenaventura: p. 4b; DavidRebata:
p. 23t; Elnavegante: p. 21b; Everett – Art: pp. 22, 27b; Vitalii Hulai: p. 17; K. Jensen: p. 31t; Julianne.
hide: p. 43b; Kaetana: p. 5; B.S.Karan: p. 7t; Kostiantyn Kravchenko: p. 43t; LiliGraphie: p. 33t;
Mountainpix: p. 6; NemesisINC: p. 19; Northfoto: p. 37; Juri Pozzi: p. 24; Lorna Roberts: p. 39; Renata
Sedmakova: p. 11; Spflaum: p. 40; IR Stone: p. 33b; Kuttelvaserova Stuchelova: p. 21t; Maksim Toome:
p. 41; Liliya Vantsura: p. 4c; Gorbash Varvara: p. 32; Wavebreakmedia: p. 42; Vladimir Wrangel:
p. 8; Wikimedia Commons: pp. 9t, 15; B. Altman & Co.: p. 27t; Andrea Appiani: p. 30; Daniel Bachler:
p. 25; Bain News Service: p. 34; François Boucher: p. 23b; Fabien Dany - www.fabiendany.com: p. 10;
Don English; Paramount Pictures: p. 35b; Marcus Gheeraerts the Younger: pp. 1, 17t; formerly attributed
to George Gower: p. 16; Jean-Pierre Houël: p. 26; Petar Miloševic: p. 14; Pattych: p. 12; Dante Gabriel
Rossetti: p. 31b; Peter Paul Rubens: p. 18; R. Sayer & J. Bennett: p. 28; Llann Wé: p. 38; Time Inc.,
Metro-Goldwyn-Mayer photograph by Harvey White: p. 35t.

Printed in the United States of America

CPSIA compliance information: Batch #CS18GS:
For further information contact Gareth Stevens, New York, New York at 1-800-542-2595.

-CONTENTS-

Chapter 1

ANCIENT
- MAKEUP -

Makeup is as old as humanity. Since prehistoric times, men and women have painted their faces as makeup has gone in and out of fashion.

No one knows when people started wearing makeup—but it was very early in human history.

MAGICAL COLOR

Some of our oldest prehistoric ancestors seem to have used makeup to protect themselves as they hunted animals and gathered roots and berries. They painted their faces and bodies with color to give them a feeling of security. Perhaps they believed that they could capture some of the power of the sun by painting their skin yellow. Or people may have believed that painting designs on their faces would scare off any enemies they might meet— or any evil spirits. **Neolithic** people buried their dead with red ochre, so the color was probably thought to have a magical power. Colored skin helped to protect both the living and the dead.

Ochre was used to make a wide range of yellows, reds, oranges, and browns.

Ancient peoples also used ochre to paint designs on the walls of caves.

Makeup also had a practical purpose. As early humans' faces and bodies became less covered with hair, layers of color helped protect their skin from the wind and the sun.

The Neanderthals, close relatives of humans who lived around 50,000 years ago, also painted their faces. Archaeologists in Spain have found seashells that were used as pots to hold reddish, yellow, and black colored powders. The makeup was made from berries and clay.

DECORATION

Once early peoples settled down in permanent villages and began to develop civilizations, they began to use makeup for decoration rather than for protection. The makeup was still made from natural products such as berries and clay, but also from a range of other **minerals**. These minerals were ground into powder and then mixed with water or oil to form a paste that could be painted onto the skin. Some people pricked color into their skin to form permanent tattoos.

Dancing girls in India wore makeup from early times.

EARLY
- SOCIETIES -

Many ancient peoples loved using makeup. For example, for fashionable Egyptians, painting their faces was part of their daily routine.

The Sumerians of Mesopotamia are famous for inventing writing, the wheel, and other innovations. They were also among the first developed culture to start using makeup.

ANCIENT MESOPOTAMIA

In a 5,000-year-old Sumerian tomb near Ur, in present-day Iraq, modern archaeologists have found a pot containing blue-green malachite, a mineral used as eye shadow, and a **cosmetics** case of equipment such as tweezers. They also found lip color used over 4,000 years ago by a Sumerian queen named Schub-ad.

The Egyptians painted the eyes because they believed the eyes revealed a person's soul.

Assyrian warriors went into battle with large, square beards, pink cheeks, and dark eyeliner.

The Assyrians were descendants of the Sumerians. They painted their faces with white lead to make their skin appear paler. King Assurbanipal, who lived in the seventh century BC, wore **rouge** on his cheeks, dark paint called **kohl** on his eyes, and perfume all over his body.

After Sumer and Assyria, makeup spread through the ancient world. The Romans adopted Egyptian beauty routines into their bathing rituals. The Minoans of Crete, meanwhile, made their own makeup using beeswax, honey, olive oil, and tree **resin**.

Obsidian was so useful that it was traded over long distances in the ancient world.

to die for

Ancient peoples had no mirrors to help them apply makeup. They likely asked someone else to put it on for them. By 6000 BC, people used a smooth black stone called obsidian to make mirrors. Later, they used stone, bronze, and other metals, such as copper. This meant that they could finally check their makeup properly.

EGYPTIAN
- BEAUTIES -

Ancient Egypt was home to women whose beauty is still legendary today, such as Queen Cleopatra. But many Egyptian men used makeup, too.

Ancient Egyptians cared about their appearance. Rich Egyptians used oils, pastes, and lotions to keep their skin soft. They didn't realize that many of the cosmetics they used were slowly poisoning them.

THE EYES HAVE IT

The Egyptians believed the eyes revealed a person's soul, so both men and women used makeup to emphasize their eyes. They outlined their eyes with thick black lines. The lines were either drawn using kohl, a black powder made by grinding **antimony**, **manganese**, and **lead**, or using crushed ants' eggs. The lines extended from the corners of the eyes, making them seem larger.

This bust of Queen Nefertiti shows how a fashionable Egyptian woman looked over 3,350 years ago.

A MAKEUP ROUTINE

Egyptian women put on makeup using a "see face," or mirror. They used stone slabs called palettes to grind up minerals into powder for makeup, and kept creams and lotions in bronze jars. Popular lotions included face creams made from egg whites or quince, as well as **lead carbonate**. Women outlined their eyes in kohl, and colored the area between their upper eyelids and eyebrows using red or green eyeshadow. They applied orange lipstick, and used a yellow-red dye made from henna to color their fingernails and toenails. Putting on all this makeup took many hours— but they had slaves who helped.

Egyptians used decorated stone slabs called palettes to grind up minerals into powder for makeup.

to die for

Throughout history, wealthy people have wanted to look different from poor people. In Egypt, rich women painted their faces lily white so they stood out from people who worked outdoors. However, they used a powder of lead carbonate—a deadly poison. Kohl also contained a high proportion of lead. The mineral slowly poisoned the stylish people who wore it.

Dancers and musicians have their eyes outlined in kohl in this painting from an Egyptian tomb.

PAINTED
- FACES -

After the ancient Egyptians set a trend for glamorous makeup, the ancient Greeks adopted a more natural look.

The ancient Romans admired the Egyptian queen Cleopatra, with her highly painted face, but they also admired the natural appearance of the Greeks. Roman makeup was somewhere between the two.

PALE BUT INTERESTING

In classical Greece, around the sixth to fourth centuries BC, Greek men saw women's role as being modest homemakers. Women were expected to stay indoors, spending their time weaving clothes. Unlike women in ancient Egypt, ancient Greek women had to appear modest and pure. For makeup, they followed an approach of "less is more." To achieve the look, Greek women used a highly **toxic** mix of white lead and chalk to whiten their faces. They mixed a root from Syria called puperissium with vinegar to color their cheeks.

A servant holds up a mirror for a Roman woman to check her makeup.

They did not paint their eyes. Greek men, meanwhile, covered their bodies with oils and perfume and used rouge and lip color.

MAKEUP IN ROME

The Romans **imported** Egyptian makeup, and traded it throughout the Roman Empire. They also made their own makeup from substances such as toxic antimony for eyeliner and nontoxic wood ash and **saffron** for black-and-gold eye shadow. They showed off any blue veins in their skin by painting them with blue paint. However, freckles were considered undesirable, so the Romans lightened them using a paste of ground wheat mixed with lemon.

Jezebel sits on her throne. A "Jezebel" became a term for a **vain**, shameless woman.

hello beautiful

In the ninth century BC, a Phoenician princess named Jezebel married Ahab, the prince of Israel. Jezebel wore a lot of makeup and beautiful clothes. After she persuaded her husband to abandon the worship of an Israeli god, the Israelis condemned her as a "painted lady." She is said to have met a horrible death, having been thrown to the dogs and killed.

WAR
- PAINT -

Warriors have always painted their faces and bodies to scare their enemies and to show which side they belong to.

This pot from ancient Peru shows a Moche warrior with his face painted for battle.

Long before ancient peoples had the idea of painting their faces to look attractive, warriors painted their faces in order to appear more frightening.

ANCIENT WARFARE

From around 1200 BC, the Assyrians decided that women should cover their faces with **veils** while men, including warriors, painted their cheeks red and put on eye makeup. They also used perfume so that they smelled good as they went into battle.

Much later, the ancient Britons of northern Europe painted their faces and bodies with a blue coloring made from the woad plant. Queen Boudicca, the ruler of the Iceni tribe, fought against the Romans in Britain in AD 60. She ordered her warriors to paint their faces blue before battle. The Iceni managed to defeat the Romans twice before finally being defeated themselves.

WAR PAINT IN AMERICA

Some of the best-known warriors who painted their faces came from Native American tribes. Each band had its own distinctive markings, with shapes and symbols that had a specific meaning. The Lakota Sioux painted black stripes on their faces, for example. The stripes indicated the warrior's role. A warrior who led a war party had two black stripes running from the corner of his eye on his right cheek. Warriors did not only use makeup to scare their enemy—it was also used in ceremonial dances and religious **rituals**.

Native Americans still use traditional makeup for ceremonial occasions.

hello beautiful

In the seventh century BC, the Babylonians ruled Mesopotamia. Their king, Nebuchadnezzar, wore makeup and told his warriors to do the same. One warrior, Parsondes, complained that makeup was not manly. As a punishment, the king forced him to shave his beard and paint his face. The result was so good that Parsondes became famed as the most beautiful woman in Babylon!

Chapter 2

THE MIDDLE
- AGES -

The Middle Ages lasted from about 500 to 1500. At this time, people left their faces unpainted, their hair uncut, and their bodies unwashed. Yuck!

After the fall of Rome in 476, Christianity increased its influence throughout Europe. Christian teaching gave people a negative view of makeup.

A CHRISTIAN WORLD

Early Christian writers argued that wearing makeup showed that a person was trying to improve upon God's creation. They also claimed makeup hid a person's real face and was a form of deception, which was a sin. Using makeup to make yourself look more attractive was seen as a sign of vanity—which was another sin. Christian women could no longer paint their faces. If they dared to wear makeup, it had to look as natural as possible.

The Byzantine empress Theodora met her husband, Emperor Justinian, when she appeared in a beauty contest.

PALE SKIN

Medieval women were expected to stay indoors. Pale skin was a sign that a woman was so wealthy she never had to go outside. To remain as pale as possible, women protected their faces when outdoors with a veil. In the 1100s, Princess Zoe was reputed to be the most beautiful woman in the Byzantine Empire. She protected her skin by never going outside.

CULTURAL EXCHANGE

Cosmetics had almost vanished from Europe before they were reintroduced from an unlikely source: warfare. In 1095 European Christians launched a series of wars against Muslims in the Holy Land. These Crusades lasted nearly 200 years and failed to conquer the Holy Land. However, they did introduce new fashions in makeup. The Crusaders returned from Asia with perfume, rouge, and glass mirrors, which were common in the Islamic world. They also copied the Arabs by shaving their faces, ending the fashion for men wearing beards.

In the 1500s, Catherine de' Medici brought Italian ideas about beauty to France when she became queen there.

THE IMAGE OF
- ROYALTY -

Elizabeth I was queen of England from 1558 to 1603, a period of peace and prosperity. She gave her name to the Elizabethan Age.

While Elizabeth never married, she was still known to be vain. Like her father, King Henry VIII, Elizabeth paid great attention to making sure her appearance was perfectly "royal."

LOOKING THE PART

Elizabeth dressed luxuriously from a young age. When she was queen, she owned 80 wigs, 27 fans, and more than 3,000 dresses. It took her ladies-in-waiting four hours every day to get the queen ready. As she lost her looks, it was said that she refused to look in a mirror for the last 20 years of her life.

Like her father, Elizabeth used her appearance to project an image of power and authority.

DAMAGING MAKEUP

To cover her skin and make her appear as pale as possible, Elizabeth was painted with layers of **ceruse**. This was made from white lead mixed with vinegar. She also used ceruse to cover her neck and hands. However, the white lead meant that the ceruse damaged the skin. One Elizabethan said that it dried the flesh and warned that: "Those women who use it about their faces do quickly become withered and grey headed."

Elizabeth's appearance was completed by orange wigs, plucked eyebrows, and scarlet lips. Her eyes were outlined with kohl. Where her dress exposed her skin, the veins were outlined in blue.

Elizabeth's lips were painted with plant dye and beeswax.

to die for

The whiter a Renaissance lady's skin, the better. Some women went to great lengths to achieve a pale appearance. This included applying **leeches** to their ears. The animals would suck the blood from the womens' heads, leaving them looking deathly pale.

leech

Chapter 3

THE EARLY
- MODERN WORLD -

In the Renaissance, Europe's rulers grew more fashion conscious. They ignored church teachings and used makeup to show off their wealth and status.

After the death of Elizabeth I in 1603, cosmetics became more subtle. Male makeup was generally more subtle than female makeup. Men simply added a touch of rouge to their cheeks or color to their lips.

FRENCH STYLE

Across the English Channel in France, major changes were underway. In 1643, King Louis XIV came to the throne. During a reign of 72 years, the new king turned France into Europe's dominant political power and its undisputed leader of style and fashion.

King Louis XIII of France, the father of Louis XIV, used makeup to achieve his look.

Louis removed his **courtiers'** political power, so they spent all their time preening and following fashion. Costumes and makeup grew ever more outrageous.

WEARING PATCHES

In the 1600s an unusual beauty craze from France swept across Europe: the wearing of "patches." People began sticking small dots of black taffeta onto their faces in order to hide blemishes and scars. The patches were not harmful, but they soon became more excessive. People began to use all kinds of fabrics and shapes, such as crescent-shaped pieces of velvet or red silk stars.

A visitor to the court in Berlin in 1616 reported that ladies there were so heavily patched that they looked as if they had been in a fight. The black patches were not very flattering. From a distance they looked more like fleas and bugs stuck to people's faces—not the look their wearers were hoping to achieve!

The shape and position of patches carried messages about a woman's availability for marriage.

DEADLY
- ITALY -

Makeup in Italy could be deadly for people in the sixteenth and seventeenth centuries. Toxic face powders were just one of the dangers.

By the sixteenth century Venice was the leading city of Europe. Its location on the Adriatic Sea meant it controlled sea routes to the Middle East and Asia. As a result, every new spice and perfume coming into Europe arrived in Venice first.

VENETIAN CERUSE

Venice was the playground of the rich. Endless parties and balls took their toll on people's looks, so "more is more" became the rule for cosmetics. Heavy makeup hid the worst of the damage.

Venice had a reputation for importing the most luxurious and expensive makeup—just right for its constant partying.

to die for

In England in the late 1700s, dark eyebrows were all the rage. However, the use of lead-based cosmetics caused many women to lose their eyebrows. Instead, they made false eyebrows from mouse fur. The only problem was keeping the eyebrows glued in place. More than one woman found her eyebrows in her teacup!

Venetian ceruse was used to whiten the face and hide wrinkles. Venetian ceruse was more expensive than ordinary ceruse—but it was just as deadly. The lead in the ceruse was toxic.

INHERITANCE POWDERS

A lot of makeup was toxic, but Aqua Tofana was deadly!

For around 50 years in the seventeenth century, dressing tables in Italy were particularly dangerous. Fashionable women could buy a clear liquid called Aqua Tofana to store among their cosmetics. This was sold as "inheritance powder," and the purchaser received secret instructions on how to use it from its maker, Giulia Tofana. The bottle contained **arsenic** mixed with lead and belladonna, made from the deadly nightshade plant. Just four doses of between four and six drops of the liquid were enough to kill a man. Undetectable on the victim, the "cosmetic" was the perfect murder tool for an unhappy wife. After more than 600 women killed their husbands with arsenic poisoning, Tofana was finally arrested and executed.

THE FRENCH
- CONNECTION -

In 1682, King Louis XIV moved his court to a vast palace at Versailles just outside Paris, where he perfected his approach to fashion.

Unlike the English, who seldom bathed, King Louis XIV liked to bathe every day and he liked to smell good.

SCENT OF POWER

Perfume-making became big business. It was part of a lavish court lifestyle where appearance was everything. Life at Versailles was so boring for courtiers with no political role that they concentrated on how they looked. The king dressed in the finest clothes and powdered his hair gray, so his courtiers followed his lead. Powdered hair was all the rage for men, while women rouged their cheeks and wore bright lipstick. Being a "painted lady" in France was seen as a compliment. Across the English Channel, it was an insult.

The French queen Marie Antoinette was famous for buying lots of clothes and makeup!

SPEND, SPEND, SPEND

Although many people in France were poor, the court at Versailles grew more luxurious. Marie Antoinette, wife of Louis XVI, spent 258,000 livres on her appearance in a year—the equivalent of millions of dollars today. That bought her a huge wardrobe and every imaginable cosmetic, plus "simple" country fragrances created just for her. When the French Revolution came in 1789, such excesses led to Marie Antoinette losing her head alongside her husband, Louis XVI. The age of excess was over.

The palace at Versailles was the center of Europe's fashion scene.

hello beautiful

Madame de Pompadour was the most important of Louis XV's mistresses. A famed beauty, she set many fashion trends. She never appeared in public without her cheeks highly rouged. Her favorite shade became known as "Pompadour Pink." Even on her deathbed, her last act was to rouge her cheeks before she died.

GEISHA

It was not only Europeans who wanted to look as pale as possible. In China and Japan, there was a tradition of using makeup to whiten the skin.

The fashion for pale skins in China and Japan started early. During the second half of the sixth century, rouge, face whitener, and other cosmetics reached Japan from China. It was not until AD 692, when a Buddhist priest made a lead-based face whitener for the Empress Jito, that Japan began its own trends in cosmetics.

WHITE AS A SHEET

During the Heian Period, from 794 to 1185, Japan cut its ties with the rest of the world. Women at the Imperial Court in Kyoto created their own ideas about beauty in isolation. Their ideals included a heavily whitened face and neck, shaved eyebrows, bright red lips—and blackened teeth. The look might not have been to everyone's taste!

A geisha's even white makeup helps focus the viewer's attention on the eyes and mouth.

to die for

Geisha used the white, lead-based powder that pleased the Empress Jito for centuries, but it scarred their faces—and even killed them. The powder caused skin problems and hair loss. As their skin worsened, the geisha used more powder to cover the damage. It was only in the late 1800s that rice powder replaced the deadly lead powder, and the geisha lived to tell the story.

A geisha's **kimono** is low at the back to reveal the white paint at the nape of the neck.

THE GEISHA

The appearance of the women of the Heian court influenced the tradition of the geisha. These formal female entertainers are skilled in arts such as dance and conversation. They change their appearance and makeup as they are trained to become more senior geishas.

Geisha commonly cover their face and neck with really thick white powder, paint in black eyebrows, and wear bright red lipstick. The white powder is mixed with water and then applied by hand all over the face, including over the eyebrows and lips. The black eyebrows are then drawn in place before the red lips are drawn over the mouth.

Chapter 4

THE NINETEENTH
- CENTURY -

In the 1800s, the highly painted look was so last century. Now most women wanted a natural look, like Britain's Queen Victoria.

The 1789 French Revolution ended the kind of cosmetic fun enjoyed by the nobles and the royal family. Across Europe, countries no longer had the money to keep such extravagant royal courts.

MEN AND WOMEN

In England, the nineteenth century saw contrasting attitudes. For men, vanity was "in," and beautifully dressed "**dandies**" took center stage. They followed the lead of the style setter, Beau Brummel. Women got the short straw, because Queen Victoria, who ruled Great Britain for 64 years from 1837, did not like makeup. She did not use it and even frowned upon it.

The French Revolution introduced a complete change in attitudes toward makeup in Europe.

In the United States, a plain appearance was the way to go. This was mainly in reaction to the heavily powdered hair of Britain's King George III. He had become a symbol of **oppression** during the eighteenth century and the American Revolution (1765–1783). Following the Revolution, American appearances had become far simpler.

Department stores, like the B. Altman department store in New York City, began selling makeup to customers during the 1860s.

MAKEUP ON SALE

The little makeup Victorian women wore was still made from natural products, such as beeswax, rosewater, or belladonna. Belladonna was used to open the pupils and make the eyes appear larger—even though it was deadly poisonous.

People no longer had to make their own cosmetics at home. Now cosmetics could be bought at the pharmacy. By the 1840s, many drugstores in the United States employed a cosmetician. They didn't just advise women about makeup. They also covered up the black eyes of men who had been injured in fights. The first "making-up" department appeared in B. Altman's store in New York City in 1867. Assistants taught women how to apply rouge, powder, and eye makeup in a subtle and natural way.

As a young woman, Queen Victoria was considered a great beauty. She later lost her interest in fashion.

[27]

THE DANDY

The nineteenth century saw two types of ideal male figure in a fight to the death: the dandy in one corner and the action-man in the other!

An early form of dandy, called the Macaronis, had exaggerated hairstyles.

The dandy saw physical appearance as everything. Just as women were having to embrace the natural look with pale skin and just a hint of rouge, men appeared so perfect they were anything but natural.

THE DANDIES

The leading dandy was Beau Brummel, a friend of the Prince Regent, the heir to the British throne. Beau never appeared in public without being perfectly groomed. He claimed to spend five hours a day **coiffing** his hair, applying paste to his face to conceal blemishes, and shaping his eyebrows until he looked perfect. The Prince Regent ditched his heavy makeup and copied Beau—and everyone else copied the heir to the throne.

ACTION-MEN

The Napoleonic Wars fought between Great Britain and Napoleonic France from 1803 to 1815 set a new male fashion. Men in uniform were everywhere. The slightly feminine dandy was replaced by a more "rugged" look. In Great Britain, the new popular heroes were the admirals, generals, and soldiers who were fighting the French. At home, men started to copy these action-men and stopped wearing pastes and face paints. Instead they set out to look more "masculine": beards and mustaches were back in and makeup was out.

The Prince Regent later became King George IV of Britain.

to die for

Across the Atlantic Ocean, American men had already moved away from the powdered and perfumed look, and had completely rejected cosmetics. In fact, the Americans' distrust of makeup was so strong that if a man used it, his reputation could be ruined. When it was discovered that the eighth president, Martin Van Buren, used cosmetic creams, the scandal helped end his political career.

PAINTED
- LADIES -

For women in nineteenth-century Britain, actresses and bohemians took on Queen Victoria in the makeup stakes. Who would win?

Queen Victoria's hatred of makeup was so great that she condemned painted faces as vulgar and unladylike. Many people seemed to agree with her.

NATURAL LOOK

Most women tried to appear as if they wore barely any makeup. The French Empress Josephine, wife of Emperor Napoleon, spent hours applying her makeup to make it look as if she wasn't wearing any! Pale skin was fashionable. It implied wealth because pale-skinned women did not go out to work. Women paled their faces with chalks and powders and stayed out of the sun. They got a little color by pinching their cheeks to draw blood into the skin.

Empress Josephine was one of Europe's most famous beauties.

FACE PAINTING

By the end of the nineteenth century, everything had changed. Actresses had worn makeup for centuries, but the stage had been seen as **disreputable**. Now, however, the theater became fashionable. Even respectable women wanted to wear makeup to look like famous actresses, such as Sarah Bernhardt. As the century ended, **commercial** makeup became widely available. In 1884, the French company Guerlain produced the first lipstick. Made from deer fat, beeswax, and castor oil, it was wrapped in silk paper so it did not color the user's fingers.

By 1900, bolder colors of makeup were back in style.

hello beautiful

From the mid-1800s, **Pre-Raphaelite** artists painted models such as Jane Morris and Lizzie Siddal, with tumbling hair, pale faces, and painted lips. This began the "Romantic" look that has never gone out of fashion since. Cosmetics gave a natural appearance that thousands of women copied.

Chapter 5
THE TWENTIETH
- CENTURY -

*When Queen Victoria died in 1901,
so did her disapproval of makeup.
Thanks to changes in the United States,
cosmetics were soon everywhere.*

From early in the twentieth century, it was clear that the United States would lead the way in all things cosmetic. Before the United States took control, however, other forces were in play.

ALL CHANGE

In 1909 a modern Russian dance group called the Ballet Russes arrived in Paris. With the dancers' brightly colored costumes and painted faces, the Russian ballet caused a storm. Their modern look was an instant hit. A few years later in Great Britain, women marching for the right to vote caused outrage by wearing red lipstick. Until recently, lipstick had only been worn by actresses and other disreputable women. It was clear that the Victorian age was long gone.

Young American women known as **flappers** broke the rules with their short hair and bright lipstick.

THE MODERN ERA

The place of modern makeup was cemented by flappers in the United States in the 1920s. These young women broke many rules. Not only did they wear short skirts and bob their hair, but they also openly wore makeup. Since World War I (1914–1918), many women had worked and earned their own money. They wanted something to spend it on—such as makeup. Companies produced cheap cosmetics that working women could afford. Alongside the chain stores' makeup counters, beauty parlors opened. Suddenly, makeup was big business—and so it would remain.

World War I was the first time many women began to work outside the home.

Makeup departments have a prominent position in modern department stores.

HOORAY FOR
- HOLLYWOOD -

During the 1930s and 1940s, many women wanted to look like Hollywood movie stars. The first giant cosmetics firms promised to help them.

Actors and actresses had worn makeup on stage for thousands of years. The makeup helped to emphasize the expressions on their faces. As black-and-white movies began, suddenly actresses were projected on screens that made them appear 10 feet (3 m) tall. They wore makeup to help them look good at such large sizes!

THE SILVER SCREEN

Everything about the movie stars was larger than life—including their makeup. Stars such as Clara Bow wore dark makeup, with heavily lined eyes and dark cupid-bow lips, which worked well on screen. Women tried to copy the look. They flocked to the beauty salons of new cosmetics companies such as Elizabeth Arden, Helena Rubenstein, and Max Factor.

Alice Joyce was a movie star of the 1910s and 1920s.

ESCAPE FROM REALITY

When the **Great Depression** began in 1929, life became tough for many people. One of the most popular ways to escape from real life was a trip to the movies. Watching glamorous movie stars with their immaculate makeup inspired women to treat themselves when they could. These small treats helped keep up their spirits. In London, 1,500 times more lipsticks were being sold in 1931 than they had been a decade earlier.

hello beautiful

Makeup gave people a chance to re-create a little of the glamour of stars such as Jean Harlow.

Marlene Dietrich (right) and Greta Garbo were Hollywood stars famed for their beauty. Garbo was the first star to use a line of kohl to emphasize her eyes. Dietrich made her own kohl from the head of a burned match that she mixed with oil. Both stars' eyebrows were thin and arched and started a huge fashion trend.

AVON
- CALLING! -

In 1886 a man launched a new service that transformed how women bought makeup. It also gave lots of women a career.

David McConnell sold books door-to-door in New York City. He began giving housewives a free perfume sample so they would agree to listen to him. He soon noticed that his customers were not interested in the books—they just wanted the perfume.

HOME-SALES SUCCESS

McConnell launched the California Perfume Company (renamed Avon in 1939). McConnell's company was the world's first home-selling makeup business. When it started in 1886, women were reluctant to buy makeup from a store. Makeup was still seen as being scandalous. Only a few years earlier, a Madame Rachel of Bond Street in London had **blackmailed** women who bought face powders from her.

Teenagers take a class in how to apply makeup in the 1950s.

ON YOUR DOORSTEP

McConnell's genius was to allow women to buy products in the privacy of their homes. This was especially important in a period when the fear of social disapproval generally mattered more than it does today. McConnell also realized that women would likely buy more from a woman than a man. He persuaded a New Hampshire widow named Mrs. Albee to work for him. She became the very first Avon lady. Many thousands of others followed her into selling makeup. Today, Avon's sales are falling. This reflects a different world. For many modern women, part of the fun of buying new makeup is trying it out with the help of an expert at a beauty counter in a department store.

Despite changing markets, Avon still has branches around the world.

to die for

In 1906, an African American woman named Sarah Breedlove opened a business selling her own hair products and cosmetics. She used the name Madam C.J. Walker. Unlike many cosmetics at the time, hers did not try to lighten black skin. Walker's skill at marketing made her one of the first successful African American entrepreneurs—and a millionaire.

POWER
- OF POP -

Makeup and rock and roll go together like peanut butter and jelly. And some male rock stars have worn far more makeup than women!

When Little Richard had a hit with "Tutti Frutti" in 1956, he was in full makeup. The singer used flamboyant eyeliner, eyebrow pencil, and lip color—and changed the face of rock and roll.

ON STAGE

Rock stars who followed in the 1960s often wore makeup, including the Rolling Stones' Mick Jagger. Wearing makeup on stage really took off in the 1970s with David Bowie. Bowie's painted appearance paved the way for later male stars such as Alice Cooper, Prince, and Kiss.

Each member of the rock band Kiss has his own black-and-white makeup design.

to die for

Goth music had its own look. Goths often painted their faces white and wore heavy makeup, from highly painted eyebrows to thick eye makeup and lips that could be any color from black to white. Goth makeup was stylized, polished, and edgy—and went perfectly with the dark music.

ESCAPE FROM REALITY

For the punks of the late 1970s, makeup was almost as important as the music. Punks favored a hard, aggressive look. That meant black everything—eyeliner, lip color, and hair color. Their look was often pulled together with many face piercings. The New Romantics of the 1980s preferred a painted face. They often whitened their faces to resemble Japanese geisha. Artists such as Duran Duran saw their faces as canvases on which to paint. Adam Ant, for example, copied Native American war paint.

Singer Amy Winehouse used kohl to enlarge her eyes and had a retro "beehive" hairstyle.

Chapter 6
THE TWENTY-FIRST
- CENTURY -

Today, the beauty industry is a global business valued at $445 billion. With sophisticated advertising campaigns and marketing, it reaches everywhere.

In 1918, Max Factor came up with the Color Harmony Revolution. He was the first man to realize that different palettes of makeup would go better with different colors of hair. Makeup has come a long way since then. There is now makeup for every ethnic group, for different ages, and for both sexes.

TRENDING TODAY

Modern makeup is so hi-tech that its ingredients resemble something from a chemistry lab. Japanese innovators led the way in high-tech makeup by experimenting with color and texture in the late 1900s. Today, US and British makeup brands use chemicals that are more typically found in medicine or car paint, such as **silicone** and **mica**. Since the late 1990s, silicone oil has often been added to makeup to make it last longer. Meanwhile, mica is a sparkling mineral

Some contemporary women rarely leave the house without at least a little makeup.

that gives a new car its added sparkle—and also makes eye shadow appear to shimmer.

TOMORROW'S MEN

Many modern men are just as concerned about their appearance as previous generations of men have been throughout history. Like men from earlier times, some are experimenting with wearing makeup, including eyeliner and eye shadow, lipstick, and face powder.

In Victorian England, men wore more makeup than women, but in the early twentieth century male makeup became **taboo**. When rock stars first started to wear makeup on stage in the 1960s and 1970s, there was public outrage. Today, male grooming is such big business that makeup has come full circle.

Cosmetic companies are starting to create makeup lines just for men. The next big thing in male makeup is predicted to be men-only makeup counters in department stores. Perhaps the dandy will be back in fashion again!

Male grooming is a rapidly growing market for cosmetics firms.

WHAT'S
- INSIDE? -

Like the first makeup, modern makeup uses natural ingredients. But some of these ingredients are actually quite disgusting!

Manufacturers set out to develop products that last and that are easy to apply. Making lipsticks from castor oil and wax does not make financial sense in the modern marketplace, because such ingredients go bad quickly. Unexpected ingredients that appear in makeup today include fish scales, grease from sheep's wool, and whale vomit!

YUCK!

Beauty companies spend millions of dollars on research and development. They try out new and unusual ingredients. A substance called ambergris, for example, is a very expensive ingredient used in perfume. It is actually protective oil from a whale's belly that the whale has thrown up. It is called ambergris because the name sounds a whole lot better than whale vomit!

A lipstick slides on easily because it contains fatty cells from sheep and other woolly mammals.

IT CONTAINS WHAT?

Lanolin is a standard ingredient in modern makeup. It helps products such as lipstick and eye shadow glide on. This is because lanolin is made from wax and dead fatty cells secreted by woolly mammals, such as sheep. Another revolting product that used to be common in eye makeup and lipstick is squalene, a gooey oil taken from the livers of sharks. Although squalene is no longer used, parts of other fish are. Fish scales add a sheen to nail polish. Just scrape the scales off a dead fish, suspend them in alcohol, then use them in cosmetics. At least fish scales are not toxic! Perhaps the age of terrible and toxic makeup is finally over.

Fish scales help make nail polish sparkle — like the pretty fish themselves.

to die for

One fashion that seems to have died is Japanese tooth blackening. The Japanese once saw black teeth as a sign of beauty. To stain their teeth, the Japanese dissolved iron filings and **tannins** from tea in vinegar. They painted the resulting mixture on their teeth. Some people believed that black teeth warded off evil spirits and brought good luck.

-TIMELINE-

c. 50,000 BC   Neanderthals use shells as holders for pigments used as makeup.

c. 4000 BC   Cosmetics are in widespread use in Sumer and ancient Egypt.

c. 1500 BC   Women in China and Japan begin to paint their faces white and paint their teeth black or gold.

c. 1330 BC   Queen Nefertiti is a beauty icon in ancient Egypt.

c. 1200 BC   Assyrian women wear veils, while warriors wear makeup to go into battle.

c. 900 BC   The Phoenician princess Jezebel becomes renowned for her fashionable clothes and painted face.

500s BC   The ancient Greeks adopt a modest, natural-looking appearance for women.

69 BC   Cleopatra is born in Egypt; she will become a famous beauty of the ancient world.

AD 1   Makeup is so common in Rome that the writer Plautus comments, "A woman without paint is like food without salt."

AD 476   The Roman Empire is overthrown by Germanic peoples, and cosmetics largely disappear from Europe.

1095   The First Crusade begins as Christians fight Muslims for control of the Holy Land; Crusaders returning to Europe bring makeup and other fashions from Asia.

1028   Princess Zoe becomes ruler of the Byzantine Empire; she protects her skin by never going outdoors.

c. 1560   Queen Elizabeth I of England begins a fashion of using white face powder.

1616	A British visitor criticizes the widespread use of face patches in Berlin.
c. 1700	Geisha bring the fashion for white faces to a peak of popularity in Japan.
1764	Madame de Pompadour is said to apply rouge on her deathbed.
1774	Marie Antoinette becomes queen of France. She is noted for the extravagance of her appearance.
c. 1785	Beau Brummel becomes leader of the dandies in London.
1789	After the French Revolution, royalty and the nobles lose their role as leaders of fashion.
1840s	Drugstores in the United States increasingly hire cosmeticians.
1837	Victoria becomes queen of Britain. Despite being a noted beauty in her youth, she later turns against the use of cosmetics.
1867	The B. Altman store in New York City introduces the first "making-up" department.
1884	Guerlain in France makes the first commercial lipstick.
1886	US salesman David McConnell founds a door-to-door company to sell makeup. It later becomes known as Avon.
1918	Max Factor introduces the Color Harmony Revolution, matching makeup tones to the color of a woman's hair.
1920s	Young American women known as flappers wear makeup and have their hair cut short.
1956	Singer Little Richard has his first hit. He performs in full makeup.
1989	Men's makeup begins to become more popular.
2006	For his spring/summer fashion show, designer John Galliano makes up his models with white faces.

-GLOSSARY-

antimony a silver-white semi-metal

arsenic a highly poisonous element

blackmailed demanded money in return for not revealing damaging information

ceruse a pigment or cosmetic made from white lead

coiffing styling or arranging hair

commercial related to buying and selling of goods

cosmetics substances that are applied to the skin, especially the face, to improve the appearance

courtiers people at a royal court who act as companions to a king or queen

dandies men who pay excessive attention to their appearance

disreputable having a reputation for poor character and morals

flappers fashionable young women in the 1920s who broke the rules of accepted behavior and appearance

Goth a style of rock music with dark lyrics

Great Depression a worldwide period of economic slowdown and high unemployment in the 1930s

imported shipped goods from one country into another

kimono a long, loose Japanese robe

kohl a black powder widely used as eye makeup in the ancient world

lead a soft, heavy metal

lead carbonate a white salt made from lead and carbon dioxide

leeches bloodsucking worms used in some medical treatments

manganese a hard gray metal

mica a shiny mineral found in rocks

minerals natural nonorganic substances, such as crystals and salts

Neolithic relating to the later part of the Stone Age, when people used weapons and tools

ochre an earthy pigment that usually contains clay

oppression a situation in which people are denied their rights

Pre-Raphaelite a member of a group of nineteenth-century English artists who tried to paint simply, like painters in the early Renaissance

resin a sticky substance released from the bark of some trees

rituals solemn religious ceremonies

rouge red powder or cream used to color the cheeks or lips

saffron an orange-yellow coloring made from crocus flowers

silicone an artifical substance used to make rubber and plastics

taboo a social custom against a particular action

tannins bitter-tasting organic substances that occur in some plants

toxic poisonous

vain having excessive pride in one's own appearance

veils pieces of fine material worn by women to cover their faces

-FOR MORE INFORMATION-

BOOKS

Baum, Margaux, and Margaret Scott. *Fashion and Clothing*. New York, NY: Rosen Publishing, 2017.

Gourley, Catherine. *Flappers and the New American Woman: Perceptions of Women from 1918 through the 1920s*. Minneapolis, MN: Twenty-First Century Books, 2008.

Higgins, Nadia. *Brilliant Beauty Inventions*. Minneapolis, MN: Lerner Publishing Group, 2013.

McKissack, Patricia and Frederick. *Madam C.J. Walker: Inventor and Millionaire*. Berkeley Heights, NJ: Enslow Publishers, 2013.

Webb, Sarah Powers. *Marie Antoinette: Fashionable Queen or Greedy Royal?* North Mankato, MN: Capstone Press, 2015.

WEBSITES

A History of Cosmetics from Ancient Times
www.cosmeticsinfo.org/Ancient-history-cosmetics
Check out this timeline to learn more about the history of makeup.

Ancient Egypt for Kids
egypt.mrdonn.org/kohl.html
This page explains how kohl was used by the ancient Egyptians.

Tudor Makeup
www.dkfindout.com/us/history/tudors/tudor-makeup/
Find out more about the makeup the Tudors wore here.

Publisher's note to educators and parents: Our editors have carefully reviewed these websites to ensure that they are suitable for students. Many websites change frequently, however, and we cannot guarantee that a site's future contents will continue to meet our high standards of quality and educational value. Be advised that students should be closely supervised whenever they access the Internet.

-INDEX-